Reveille

Reveille

poems

by

Michael Nipert

Book and cover design: VertVolta Design

Cover image: 'Sun Clouds' ⓒⓒ Bureau of Land Management, via Flicker.com

ISBN: 979-8-9909921-0-8

Published by

Michael Nipert, Seattle WA

michaelnipert.com

To my three sons, Byron, Alex, and Scott,
who made this pilgrimage with me.

Contents

THE RISING LIGHT

ONENESS

The Broken Thread

The Order

I met him at Fiore Café
one late muggy afternoon where
I was working on a short story
and drinking too much coffee
struggling to keep my eyes
from drifting off to sleep.
He sat next to me at a large round table.
His hair and eyes were dark like mine
and his face looked back like a mirror.

"What are you writing," he asked?
and he looked straight through my eyes
which left me feeling a little unsettled.
"It's a story about freedom
and the divinity of the child,"
I hesitantly replied.
"Those are good themes," he said.
I nodded then turned my head
and buried myself back in my story

Moments later he reached out
with strong calloused fingers
and gently touched me on the shoulder.
"I have a story for you, he told me,
if you would like to hear it.
It's about a dream I had,"
he blurted out abruptly.

"You might want to write it down."
Dreams, I thought, you should
save your dreams for your therapist,
but I was stuck sitting next to him
and felt oddly compelled to listen.

"Seven nights," the stranger recounted,
"in one summer the same dream.
My first child had just been born in March
and I had begun to see the presence
of some insidious force growing with arrogance
in the news, the universities, and on the streets.

In the eerie repetition of the dream
I found myself again and again
jumping on a train in the mountains
where I had hid with a band of renegades
up in the cold caves of the Cascades.

The Order, as they called themselves,
had killed most of the rebels,
as they purged each trace of dissent.
They were harsh and surgical
with their ideological operations.
I had been told that they
had gathered all the children
and sequestered them by age
in prisons across the state.

I had heard about the training,
programmatic hypnosis and shock therapy,
and my only child, my infant son, was locked up
in one to be sterilized of any memory of me
and our dire attempts to hold onto agency
and the last few flames of humanity.

With each visitation of the dream,
I rode the cold rumble of steel
into the shrill quiet of the valley.
Guards stood perched at every station;
suspicion peered from every eye.
Like dogs on a leash, they sniffed
the air for the scent of freedom.

I entered the prison in Monroe
where I was sure they had taken my son.
With ropes I climbed to the roof
where a hatch on the tallest building
opened to a series of internal ladders
that led to the ground floor.
I had been shown the prints
that the others had gathered
as they wrestled with plans
to liberate the children.

In stealth I wandered the halls
until I heard a concert of voices
forming their mouths around slogans.
I entered a large gymnasium
where all eyes were mesmerized
by a huge commanding screen.
When I saw my son, I was able
to approach undetected and slipped
him through the double door
and fled as fast as I could
to the room where the ladders
led to hope and our escape.

I placed my boy in a backpack
and ascended the first few rungs
when a guard with a gun burst
into the room and pointed it
at my head and shouted at me
to climb back down to the ground.

The next few steps happened so quickly;
they continue to this day
to unfold in my mind as a blur.
Backhanding the guard in the face,
my fingers felt like steel claws
as I ripped back through his trachea
with one deft and swift movement.

I murdered the same man
seven times that summer, seven times,
the same way, the same man,
blood spurting in gushes to the floor,
the hasty ascent up the ladder,
repelling on ropes down the wall,
the piercing whistles and sirens blaring.

The escape once my feet hit the ground
occurred differently every time: gunfire,
rolling through fields, dodging bullets,
hiding in ditches, waiting for the train
to carry us back to the mountains.

As I reflected on these nightmare visions,
the one thing I knew I would not do
was let my son and my future children
be taken and conditioned by some new
gauntlet of moral authority where dialogue

and difference are driven deep underground,
where the wings of imagination
are clipped and bound in a cage,
where the growth of human inquiry
spurns the spirit of love and compassion,
where fear is the first impulse with each
moment we begin to say what we see.

I promised myself that summer
that I would raise them to be free,
that I would fight for their autonomy
on every uttered ground I stood.
For freedom is the only way to feel
and see the infinite and holy in the word.

Seven times that dream came for me
in one summer so many years ago
rumbling through my brain
like the train heading back
into the valley to snatch
my son from their grasp.

I have thought of it many times,
as it has slowly come to pass.
The Order is closing upon us;
it's time to wake up," he said,
and he rose to his feet
and he touched me one more time
on my shoulder and walked
out the door and did not look back
as he seemed to just disappear
out where I stared into the clear air.

A Singular Identity

I'm calling poetry back again,
back from the dark recess.

I'm not sure what to name you
this time – as distant as you are.

The way I've known you before:
raven's hair and witchcraft,

the invisible delight of another
language beyond this world,

the lavender light teasing me
out of the illusion of flesh.

I thought I would hatch from
human concern and melt my feathers

into the thunder of your throat,
the thrum of your veins.

Lost in the folds of your body,
mad in the winds of your hair,

I would speak like no other
in a charred tongue of ecstasy.

These passions have grown faint in me,
all too human with my concerns.

I feel the mold of physical decay
and the gravity of money,

and the father of the fathers
has shackled me to a stone.

I listen for the heartbeat in the ground,
feel the struggle of the others,

voices trapped in the rumble
of wheels on endless streets,

the lost feet pacing the sidewalks
looking through shop windows

for an image to praise,
for a mannequin to call their own.

And there is so much pain
when you really love someone.

I've heard and know there must be
some other way of letting go,

other than the indifference
that settles like dust on every

counter, tongue, and shelf.
First of all we must open

up again to the many
and the pain beginning

to rush over us like
powerful ocean wave on stone.

And what we thought was us
will be formed by the great hands

of the other, and what we felt
irreparable in our hearts

will turn on that great lathe
into a beginning of a love

that has no condition – happiness
or ecstasy – but rather embraces

and asks for something other
than the forceps to pull

the head back through
the rabbit hole of recognition.

I am waiting for this vision
to filter into me

saturate my body with
open air – erase my fears.

A singular identity
will be the end of me.

A Homeless Poem

This is a poem that needs a home;
it wanders the streets coatless
and alone in the rain.

The gray bellied clouds above
show no mercy and unfold
in flurries of indifference.

Sleeping in snatches anywhere
it can get warm and dream,
this is a poem that wanders

the bus stations and alleys,
pinching change from pedestrians
on the sidewalks and public squares,

struck by the indifference of nearly
everyone everywhere, a quarter
here, a dollar there to appease

the conscience in the mirror
of each shop window where
they purchase their pleasure.

This is a poem of boney ribs
and unwashed faces and hair,
of the delirium tremens,

of devastating addiction
and friendless uncertainty
of imminent danger everywhere.

This is a poem that has lost its way,
everyday a struggle just to eat
and find some fix to forget
the defeat and the rough road
back to who they were
when they woke to the world

from the mother's womb
to the dark tomb of night
to the memory of the light.

This is a poem that doesn't care
for the American dream anymore
and all its frenetic affairs,

piss puddles on the pavement,
the curse of the bottle,
the curse of money everywhere.

This is a poem without a home
who wanders to nowhere,
where nobody really cares.

Howl Street

What my eyes have seen on Howl Street,
a half a year deep in the neighborhood,
the midnight muddy boots of cops
on my stairway, a flashlight
penetrating the depth of my sleep.
Through the delirium, questions, a story,
a woman held hostage someplace near,
my son apologizing for opening the door,
my Baby confirming that it is not her.

Out on Martin Luther King Way,
nine policemen huddled with rifles and pistols
behind the red fence ready to fire,
eyes in the window, hush in the air,
my black wolf dog climbing over the gate
bursting out on the loaded street
just to see what she could smell.
Only a month or so since two carloads
of young men poured from their doors
and sprinted through the alleys and streets
hot on the scent of someone's last breath.
When they left sideways through the corner,
they fired a round of lead into the heart of his house.

And just today an adolescent boy
pulled from his car and thrown
on his chest and face with six patrol cars

for protection; no answers to our questions.
In a few minutes everything disappeared.

This valley hangs like a noose
in the balance, and the police
it's hard to say how far they might go
just to touch the violence they can feel.

This hillside view on one street only
of the war on poverty
of blood on blood
is a word to be read in the context
of the others, street by street,
nation by nation, race by religion,
until the hour of our death. Amen.

Number Thirteen

After so many centuries of struggle and escape,
I'm not yet sure how to flee from what comes next.
I woke up under water; I thought it must be a dream,
so I started kicking like a tadpole until I took on another shape.
I was confined in a tree, like Ariel, for what seemed like many years.
I would bend in the wind and creek like old bones,
whistle through the knotholes, but no matter how hard I tried,
not a single word was uttered so I could be understood.

Now it may have been my own spirit, or perhaps
you could say Prospero set me free, but I escaped
that tree and fell like a leaf into the face of a child.
I woke up crying and kicking, sticking and thrashing.
Pretty soon I was crawling out of my crib and down
an elongated hall; the open door where light streamed
through from a spill of yellow called me to my feet,
and I stumbled into a run until I thought I was a butterfly
circling the sun like Icarus, when I fell again and again;

each time I became the prisoner of some new scheme.
I turned to stone when I found religion. I made pyramids
with my hands for several lifetimes, and after the Inquisition
was over, I worked for Ford and the right for riches.
I broke my back and broke my back again until
I cracked open and began to meditate on a new plan -
on how a man can learn to be free or how a man can learn to be.

The sun sat down beside me; the wind wrapped around
me like a shawl. I licked the honey from my lips
and started flapping once again, almost forgetting
the shame I had felt when they branded me with a number.

Elephant Jumble

Elephants jumble the jigsaw
puzzle as they gently stomp
and parade across a glass table

I try to imagine some way of stopping
them fearful that the glass might break
and of course of the scattering
but they have no care or sense
for what I had assembled

the pieces like shards of glass themselves
impossible to swallow difficult to hold
brought together into some order

where I could somewhat make out
the color of the sky and the position
of a castle on the horizon

and what I saw coming over the hills
hordes of angry people their people
stricken down next to next
uninoculate inarticulate horde
stricken down by a plague of blindness
and the excruciating emptiness of hunger

Who let the elephants out to romp
across the day this way

just when I was beginning
to be able to say what should
and what just might happen

Oh if but we could…
keep our concentration together
the thousand pieces appropriately placed
who would ever imagine
that the many would submit

to no shelter or care
their children unfed unfit
to thrive anywhere but under the whip
or in a dungeon or a strait-jacket

I saw hordes rising
with fits of rage
in the fruitless pits
of their stomachs

when I heard the rumble
of the giant hooves entering the room
and a snicker from up in the castle

Sisyphus

I

Sisyphus rolls the unforgiving rock up the steep
hefts heaves talks to himself sopped in sweat
kills regret with something less than hope
some unrelenting stretch to reach the top.

The people below in their lantern houses
murmuring together about the weather
or a trip to Cabo or their cabin on the island,

or the children under the bridge casting dice
and scrapping for bread or the young men
in their fever breaking into the huddled homes
or stores or banks or even the walking dead
addicted to the needle and the broken thread
all feel the inevitable rumble and crush
all live in its dark shadow.

II

The grunt struggle to rise above the weight below
the dust and rubble of cathedral and tower
the children who could not ford the river
lost to circumstance lost to drugs
the lovers who have faded like a dream
from the touch, cut like a flower at the stem,
the madness of money and the smugness of power

Sisyphus stirs in each and every one
to shoulder the boulder upward again

III

Unlike the oblivion of birth
there is the memory of repeated failure
the impossibility of balancing something so prone
to rolling over to the other side of itself
as a word or a creed or rounded stone
and there are the echoes squawking magpie
through the valley that the gods
have ordained this fate for him
that the rock is a punishment
for chaining down death
or relishing the sweets of life too much.

IV

When Sisyphus reaches near the summit
and the sun saunters over the jagged peak
and the snowbirds return to whistle through the branches
and the people below rise from their sheets
to write with their wills in the scrolls of possibility
and Cain turns to Abel and offers up his crop
and the prodigal son knows his home again
and is not far off Sisyphus alone remembers
with his blisters against the cold stone

that death again will come
that some will burn with rage and hunger
that the best of the children may go unfed
that the damn rock will roll right
back down into the pit as the gods
or some principles of unevenness have fated it.

V

You might think he'd just throw
his hands up and quit
the rumbling boulder thrashing through
the bushes houses banknotes and friends
and yet he returns again and again
with ardor to the struggle
for the spinning world to stop
for just one half-formed thought to pass
between the agony of ascent
and that slow shrug back into the bottom
the heart like the first crack of light
before it spills out a scourge of bees
the unfolding of the blood blistered hands
palms up into pure possibility.

Paradoxical Birth

If this is like a dream,
the corporeal drum of the heart,
the will attempting to assert itself
over the inimical forces –
pure illusion – time/space –
the contortions of a contortionist,
who then imagined this grand fiction,
these incomplete actors
in a half-conceived farce?
Perhaps it's merely a dream
of that big dreamer
that cosmos headed reveler
who sleeps to wake
beyond the half-baked images
that wander helpless in the ghetto
valley beneath existence.

If we never happened,
like you and me never
really coming together to complete
the unutterable union of being,
if we are like an Escher hand
drawn on the white page
struggling to sketch itself
into corporeal flesh

and if this stuff of the sensual flux
is merely a diminishment of the true
matter beyond earth, water, fire, and air,
like Arjuna's vision of God in the Gita,
then perhaps our persistent desire
for transcendence and inward vision
just might bring some clarity
to the rumblings of the dream,

a solitary discernment to see through
the conflicts between opposites,
and the peristaltic process that sifts
the grist from pure existence.

Solitary Soul

We have been under months
of sweltering sun in Seattle
Even the shadows sweat and complain

The streets are empty
of sorcery; everyone is trying
so hard to be somebody

All the young men hide
behind beards and the young women
with their yoga matts and jogging shoes
parade before the mirrors until sleep
sweeps them up to repeat
the day in their dreams

I am waiting for an original
thought to step up and sit down
next to me – for a face that is not
already in the program for the evening
to smile without pretense
and waver into electricity

An original act or thought or dream
must have some permanence
beyond all this mimicry

Of course what is new
and stunningly alive
like everything else will fade and die
Even if it's Homer or Shakespeare
the shelf life is never forever

Yet to me these moments
as you have written
with you walking the dry path
into the blonde hills

and the grasses blending
in the dusk with the presence
of me wrapped around you
like an evening shawl
will and will not fall
into non-existence

The world is double when
the soul is awake – singular
and part of something greater
than we can know – while
what we do and what we think
and what we think we are
cease to be continually
like the seconds of a clock
or the Heraclitian stream

Many friends a wife a fiancé
even the man I was to them
have been swept away
What has kept me on this path
unto myself as you say
unfolds from the soul
in the air above me
and through the presence
of the Friend never too far away

Polarization

Our souls are still entangled
whirling through the dark
hurtled forth through ignorance
but there still remains a spark
that flickers and falters
that calls us to explain
why we're not together
with the gift of love in flames
with the need to heal the sundering
to heal the emptiness inside
to wake the light within
that all sides may abide

When Love Abides

Who would of a person judge
by one feature or another must
remember all people are one

and all people one by one
must derive their own sensibility
from more than a single identity.

It is the good work they do,
the love of their friends and family,
the love they show for their enemy,

the growth they've come to spiritually,
their love of animals, rocks and trees.
It is the way they've learned to see.

Kindness shines with felicity.
Compassion radiates from within.
Drum beats of originality

herald our future expansion.
Who you are and who I am cannot
be determined through simple division,

through crude and spiteful reduction.
Despite what you might think justified,
each hatred tears you up inside.

We must distinguish from grave wrong
what people individually become.
Hatred is the great divide.

Love unites when love abides.

Craving for Fire

Between what I knew then
and what I know now...
the difference has become
when and how it happens.

The possibilities of the mind
throttled on the wind,
it seemed as if I would
find myself awakened one
morning to the land beyond blood,

to the blustery realm of spirit
busting out in continual creation.

They pressed like angels on my dreams.
They rose russet in the autumn leaves
They blasted sea on jagged rocks.

The beauty of strung lights
out in the endless night,
the hatch of pebble and stone,
wish and thought, into what
expanded and was begotten
into a synergy of a love
defying decay, exceeding delight,
inexpressible growth into light.

I thought this was mine by right.
Now I know how slow it goes
when we grow old and stuffed
with candy and endless spice,
lost in the numbers we memorized,
as if stuck without a lighter
in the cold and rubbing sticks together
like the men of old craving for fire
to ignite again in the heart.

What We Remember

The days march, the soggy socks
and nasal drip, the cough, the cold
and dread into the dead of winter.

What we have lost
is what we remember:

the forsythia and its yellow bloom,
the swoon under a summer moon
where we lingered long and caressed
until time slipped and slept.
We remembered to forget
and the wheels churned
the day into butter
and each step we took felt
better than the other.

We had come together lover,
family and friend for the feast,
the dance of green fluttering
in the wind, the laughter,
the sensuous button
of the rose blossoming.

What we've lost
is what we remember

on this slow slog through winter.
What we held dear and what
we can no longer hold together,
the leaves mulching
into the brown loam,
the wisdom from mouths
that can no longer utter –
that mother and father,
that mentor and brother.

We might think blinded in snow
traversing the frozen slope
that we are alone – that
our memories have left us
and slipped into the soup
of the thick fog below –

that the mouth grew numb
and all the florid words
that flourished on the tongue
were nothing more than
melody of flute and flower,
the flush of color, the rush
of river, of love, the late night

touch and talk of living together
forever above the fading prattle
of the conventional throng.

What we've lost
is what we remember

as we bang the drum of the heart
and refuse to relinquish the child
blushing in the naked spring,
the love we relished,
the feathers unfolding,
the faith in our wings,
the titillating kiss,
the talk, the song.
The soul touched the flesh
and forgot where it came from.

And now as we remember
the flotsam of the flesh
as we march and slog
through withering forgetfulness,

what we've lost that
is essential to our progress
whispers through the cold
knuckles and knees,

blows through the bare branches.
The call and echo of the soul
everywhere advances into the emptiness

and what we discover
through each leaf and lover
through late night fever
and fecund romances,
the spirit was always
an immanent blessing
even when lost and forgotten
in the sap of the senses
and the mental traps
of foolish pretenses.

What we remember is what
we've lost and what we've lost

becomes the ember of each
future endeavor beyond the flesh
and beyond the self and its
molted feather; the mystery
of spirit lives forever.

Drum Beats

Dream of the Drum

When this muse comes and knocks
on the door of my dreams, she has not come
to whisper slippery syllables in my ear
to undulate like a stream through mossy stones
to dizzy me with love or an angelic tongue.

No, this muse comes to beat the drum
and wake me from my silent slumber
make me tremble and shake my fist
in the air at the clarity of imagery
she flashes before my eyes.

The dream sweeps by a river on fire
The masters yammer in forked tongue
the infection collateral in everyone
who adheres to the envenomed word
The dream sweeps within and beyond
through thousands of broken scenes.

I can see from what flashes before me
they have come to degrade our children
and bar the birth of the unborn
who hesitate in the brooding clouds
and the loud rumble of thunder
to enter a world torn asunder by hatred.

The next scene of the dream like
an alien conquest dropped from above
or slipped through interdimensional portals
substance and form through human flesh
whistling like a wind through knotholes
and crevices in what we thought we knew

fills us with simultaneous notions
that only true agency can refute,
an invasion of insensate guile.

They don our most coveted feelings
and work them against our better selves.
They inhabit my brothers and sisters
as they march them down the desolate road
of endless war, of the madness of Mars,
so that they can harvest and control

the precious hearts and minerals
and most of all the electric souls
that have risen up from the true progress
of our quest for consciousness.

I see them as they have taken the place
of many I have known and loved.
When I speak to them and reach for them
to pluck them from the magnetic field

and call them to the light of the soul
and what we remember of each other,
they only see the imagery of what
possesses them and shakes their limbs
and curses my dissent from their mouths.

The muse that comes to beat the drum
will not allow our banished resignation
out where we wander the wilderness
uninnoculate and unanointed, out where
one can hear the lion roar in indignation
and the eagle cry for a higher love.
This muse with her hair spread wide
across the sky cries for us to awaken
and rise to the beat of the drum.
Her bugle blows at the break of dawn
and the awakened ones repeat
we must not-forever not-succumb.

The New God

The Gods have fled within
and left the sky, the earth, and sea.
Thor with his thunderous hammer
gavels the pulsing brain.
Lakshmi and Ganesha gather
data and calculate risk,
while Zeus is a swan no longer
and Krishna has fallen asleep.

A dove is just a dove and we
forget the Druidic stones and trees.
Division, hatred, fear and shame
now forge the new decree,
crafted by those God only knows
with sanctimonious morality.

Who gave them the Divine Right
to invade our consciousness thus
and slander our names with words
that twist like thorns around the brain,
to force us to submit to their
all-encompassing dream?

The flood is already upon us;
every channel is the same,
the hysterical faces flooded
with the white noise of shame.

They tell us we are born
marked and inhumane,
then ply their favorite tortures
in the new God's name.

A Howl from the Wilderness

Meandering through Woodland Park Zoo,
I came upon lemurs and tigers too.
The unique shapes of peacocks and ostriches
awakened me to the endless possibility.

Who could have guessed a more
diverse array of physical identity,
and all of them so docile, or engaged
in play; what a wonderful panoply
of color and harmony.

As I thought further, the bars
and their cages began to shrink
and their camouflage and distinct stripes
grew gray and dull and their wild roars
or howls or screeches softened
into a sleeping pill of a spell
and their differences faded
in their separate cages and after
thousands of years of such passivity,
they all became one bland and hairless creature
that walked in circles and repeated
the same thing over and over
throughout the ages trapped
inside its mental cages.

What I could see from where
my thought had taken me,
the creature who had tamed fire
and conceived the seven wonders
had long ago relinquished
the strength of the lion
and the eagles' perspective,
as it cornered itself in captivity
under the cunning design
of an oppressive collective.

Simon Says

You need to go to art school
to know how art's supposed to be.
You need your MFA to learn
the avant-garde of poetry.

You need to have your consciousness
raised to the enlightened political view.

God forbid you think for yourself.
You know that they will follow you
and lock you up inside the stocks,
or flog you with professional shame.

They'll take your soul and stretch it out
and strip you of your precious name.
They say they're bound by empathy
to punish those who disagree.

So sure of their authority,
there is no room for inquiry.
They play the game of Simon Says,
and everyone listens carefully.

They smirk and mock and flat refuse
to see what others say they see
because honestly when Simon Says,
there's only one way you can be.

Identity Crisis

As if the ground turned
to quicksand or the land
became like the sea,

everyone began panicking
and pulling each other down,

pulling each other under
easy labels to understand,

like a simple fable with only
good and evil, up and down;

then they hardened like petrified
wood into the good that could

curse and damn their enemy
or anyone who might disagree

with their hegemonic authority
with their definition of all you see

They bake and talk their trickery,
with rickety tropes and contraband,

to drown their opposition
in questionable contradictions.

Each accusation they make
makes them with greater certainty

a strong and just identity,
the truth about everybody.

Because

Your right to hate
Because I'm a man
Because I'm middle aged
and white enough
Because I don't repeat
the slogans they've crafted
to turn your head away
from the hand in your pocket
Because I don't apologize
for the privilege you imagine
Because I'm proud of my heritage
even though we were poor
Because I study the contradictions
and hold a mirror to your actions
Because I have my own faith
and it's not based on hatred
Because love is pure feeling
and not a cultural strategy
Because I speak up for freedom
and not your new religion
Because everyone is equal
on the scales in my mind
Because I love my children
and refuse their sacrifice
Because I know the love in you
beyond the spite and division

Because I agree with what is true
but resist the distortions
Because I call to your spirit
and believe in your perfection
beyond this foul infection
plaguing each of our houses

Beyond the Divide

The world is divided into two
but no longer the division
and complete inclusion
Noah sought to fill his Ark

Now it's a line
equatorial and firm
either you are black or white
either you are red or blue
either you are wrong or right

I refuse to be torn in two
My pronoun is everyone
You are me and I am you

I am father and mother
family and friend
I am at the beginning
and I am at the end
I am both and neither
I refuse the inimical
negation of the other

These hostile and fatuous
labels are the nature
of the flood and the plague
They are the fever of war

They are everything we
were not fighting for
like the love of the other
like the sun and moon
like the yin and yang
and the counterpoint tune

I am at the beginning
and I am at the end

I am not what you think you see
and am still your friend

I refuse to be divided
into either or - us and them

I am two by two into
the ark of the ache of it
through human suffering
the marriage of opposites
I am become you and you
will become me - it is our destiny

The Hydra

The Hydra hides in a green sea of obscurity
with our great throng hardly acknowledging
it's presence among us; we go about our days

slandering and pandering each other's worth.
We divide into families, religions, and factions.
We cry out our grievances and protest on the streets.

We hardly notice the head of the beast
popping up in the press, controlling universities,
manipulating our shows like a marionette.

We hardly recognize its face in the wars
that come in waves of silent succession.
The Hydra lives and breathes from within

through our spiteful division and ignorant
distraction from the war we cannot see.
This many-headed monster seeks invincibility.

Some say it is too much, too late; it has grown
too large in its ravenous campaign to make
its power complete. To bring the Hydra to defeat

we must sever its absolute thought from our heads

without just turning around and doubling down.

The Hydra hides in quiet prosperity; we will not

find it anywhere near the projected target and we

cannot forget the guile of the beast and the subtlety

we must see to cut off the golden head of our enemy.

The War

They will tell you
it has always been this way
with the rich and the poor
and the man with his whip
and the soldier in the field.

Can you imagine a child
with a stone above his head
who was born expendable?
Of course, a mother grieved
her heart in her hands
and massaged the sinews
of the broken man,

and there were those who fought
with sticks and stones, gave speeches,
wrote songs, led armies down
the midnight road to their extinction.

They will say when alone
it's just the common man.
Nature abhors a weakness
and forgives those who win.

They will say—they will say:
it's always been this way
with the masses in a trance
marching this way and that.
They remember, they forget,
they will never keep from falling
flat as shadow into their sad song.

But the war is on and the war is long.
We must remember what has been done,
our children led to the maw of the beast
and how they turned us each on each,
armies directed to the promised land.

The Following

We see a people act as one,
believe as one, know as one,
the truth to their indignation

without a single question; they rally,
protest, and condemn the others
who have the temerity to disagree.

The argument is never heard;
never a word is permitted
to parry their authority.

The narrative is all that matters,
even if the news has lied,
even if it can be proven.

The narrative must be protected.
Like dogs on a chain, they fight
whoever challenges their master,

a master they don't even know,
a master they have never seen,
but they continue to take their orders

from the internet, TV, and magazines,
their truth, the only truth they take
for gospel and moral ascendancy,

while the masters wear disguises
and roll in the money they make,
revel in their power to divide us

and recreate their mistakes.

More for War

With the call for more war,
the big gilded press in your ear
with no fear of the devastation,
the thousands of mangled children
and women and innocent men,
Muslim, Christian, whatever religion,
black, brown, yellow or white,
who could consent with such
conviction to the battle cry
of empathy, country after
country, war torn without end.

The thunder of bombs and missiles,
the rattle of rifles and pistols
with no dissent or argument,
they cry for endless infantry,
and who are we to support such
a strategic crush of humanity
in the name of exorcizing evil
from every corner of the earth,
when, in fact, we've armed them
and promoted the necessity
for more, for continuous war,
when, in fact, we just may be
our own number one enemy.

Reflection

We are everything we claim to disdain
as we lie with indignation at another's lie
We cry out for freedom of the press
and then censor and suppress our opposition
We accuse our opposition of fomenting hate
while we incite riots and collateral destruction
Our inclusive vision is built on exclusion
Our righteous virtue thrives on degradation
Our heartfelt compassion sees only ourselves
Our outrage over racism is rife with racial hate
We write our own story then refuse this right to others
We talk about justice then slander the innocent
We cry out against sexism with sexist judgment
We call others fascist then compel them to our will
We demand apologies but never admit our mistakes
We appropriate at will then condemn others who do the same
We spurn religious worship then canonize our own precepts
We plant bias in every phrase then call it out in others
We say we're aware but just repeat what we've been told
We cry out for fluidity but only on our own terms
We curse the hierarchy then defer to our experts
We define the phobias of others then fester in our own
We spit on authoritarian power then claim our supremacy
We bleed for some children then brand others with original sin
We praise our moral purity then turn on our best friend
We insist we believe in freedom but demand others submit

If we became everyone then we would all surely forget
the creativity of autonomy and the everlasting secret
to crack the code and rise above the heavy human load
If we became everyone then we would all surely forget
the alchemy of love and the soul above and beyond
this militant march toward unquestioning complicity

If Then

If you know what you want
to say like a plan that leads
you by the hand
to only one end

If you know what the truth
is supposed to be
because the professors
professed their ideology

If the taboos have changed
and dissent needs to be shamed
as your conscience turns into policy
and you have to say you agree

If poetry becomes a product
of science and psychology
and the senses and pretenses
are your only reality

If the vision of the unknown
becomes a mathematical equation
or love and friendship turn
into a measurable situation

If your education
has given you the proper script
and it makes you indignant
when someone questions it

then you cannot will not
think of anything new
cannot and will not see
even the shadow of the truth

Reveille

The great glass buildings reflect each other
and the consternation of the clouds
The bustle of the people below
has been hushed into little huddles
as the puddles fill with gray and sullen rain

I want to cry out and blow
the bugle for genius to unfold
for the spirits who have forsaken
our misbegotten road
to return in explosions of love

to crack these tiny eggshells
and coddling codes that we
might spread our wings and fly again
that the lion might be born
to roar in poetry and song

It's time to refuse to comply
to tear up their lies and rip
off our veils and become the one
we were destined to become

I hail the voice within and the spirits
that reside beyond our perception
stuck inside this grand illusion

For all those who would bind us
to their authority I spit my lines
and scoff at their divisive decrees
setting one people upon another

Throw down the bottle and dispel
the confusion with passion
and righteous indignation

We are a world we are a vision
of infinite possibility
when the respect for each other
is the right to be free

In the early morning orange glow
I can imagine more than we know
with each original rhapsody
born from that necessity
to heed the rumble from within

Coming Up

I've seen this madness
growing like a fever
growing like a fever all night

I've seen the night
getting darker and darker
with the devils coming
out in plain sight

I've heard their words
and knew where they were headed
long before they would admit it

Those who they loved
who didn't catch the fever
they ridiculed and cast
out like demons

I love my children
I love all people
even when they're lost
even when they're cruel

I know myself
that I have been blinded
and at times played
the part of the fool

I check myself often
though I am ready
We must be ready for battle

They rattle their sabers
They talk their smack
They act as if we are vermin

I know that love
is the greatest attack
when you sense evil
or an act of oppression

What comes from that
is the next step
to never lose
your human emotion

The tides are thick
with sickness and blood
with those who care
nothing for the children

I keep thinking
we can rise above
this madness
afflicting our reason

I keep thinking
we can rise above
like the sun
coming up every season

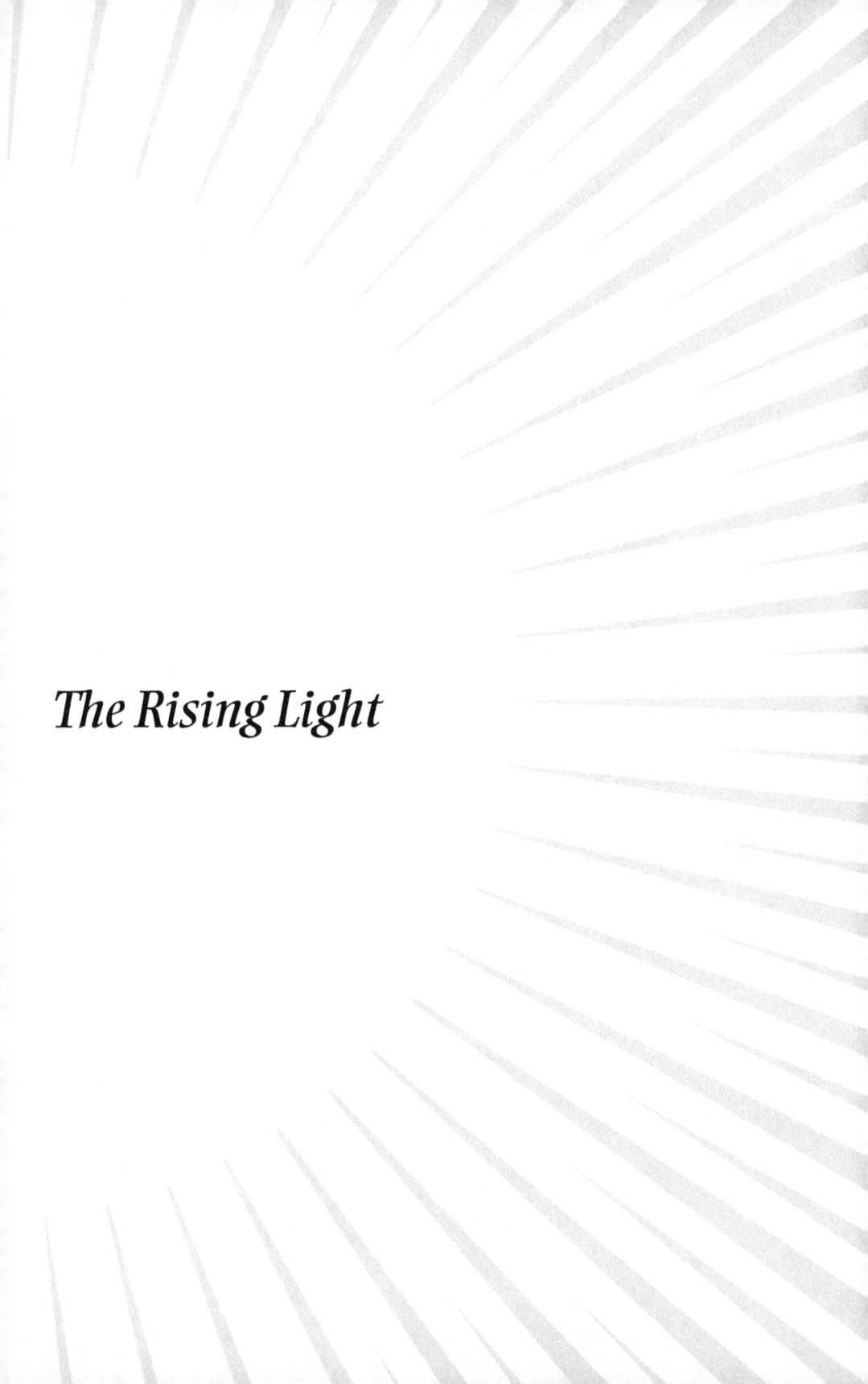

The Rising Light

The Blessing

Bless those years we've laid to rest,
the people we've known who have died
or left, the emotions we've shared,
the lips we've kissed, bless them
all for what once was us.

Bless the children who some
may curse, and bless the curse
that it is not worse.
Bless the night that grows
too long with nightmares
howling through the storm.

Bless the day the light burst through,
sun-kissed leaves and morning dew.
Oh bless those who believe in you.
Believe, believe; the love comes through.

And bless those who writhe in pain
caught on thorns or mental strain.
Those who are hungry, bless them too,
whether for power or not enough food,
not enough love, not enough pleasure,
not enough work, not enough leisure.
Caught on the plain of needing more.
just or unjust, bless the poor.

Bless the trees; bless the stones.

Bless the nights we sleep alone.

Bless the gift when it comes;

for all awaits an offering.

Bless the stars; bless the dirt.

Bless the fertile words come forth.

Bless the giver; bless your God,

for what is begotten comes from beyond.

Bless the journey of the years to come,

the sudden vistas in elevation.

Bless the struggle; bless the light.

Illuminate the dark soul's plight.

Bless the creator; bless the guide.

Bless the enemy that lives inside.

By what is given, and how we live,

let us rise through the love we give.

Orbiting Earth

How can we know this love
when it passes like noon to midnight
when after the years of moving on
it appears to be gone.

Some claim that love is always there,
everywhere ready to pour like music
into your ear, ready to twirl
like a ball on your finger,
ready to walk through the door
through the eyes of a stranger.

Love does feel like the answer,
but how do we sustain
its effervescent feeling;
how do we maintain
the connection between us?

Love confounds reason,
presses beyond mortality.
Love knocks on thin air
to pass through to eternity.

Where love has hatched
or embryonic grown,

it is as if we have awakened
beyond the realm of sticks and stones,
beyond the war of competition,
beyond the selfishness we've known.

Love is the miracle of remembering
each portal to the light,
each expansion beyond our skin –
from communion in another's suffering
to the ecstasy that is awakened
orbiting earth in a lover's arms.

Dreamtime

There is a dream
where we may meet
the jasmine and honeysuckle
the thrum of a soft drum
the whisper of a river before
the rush of the rapids appear

I see us walking beyond
our hands clutched
in the magnetic weather

of two souls rising
swallows above the wires
beyond the cloak of cloud
the blue ink ineffable

the unheard word melting
on the yellow road
until all we know
is the endlessness
we have begun
in a rush of devotion

Grace

Every new challenge that walks
through my door is a visitor
I must embrace with grace

Each rejection I've known,
each love that has flown
with florid feathers from my cage
must be so it seems to me
answered with grace

I ask myself why this is so
when a part of me cries no;
take your pound of flesh as they go.
But there is this relationship
to something more which grows
inside and opens my door wide
to the spirit I begin to know

It is thee who floods this
emptiness inside as the sun spills
it's rosy red elixir over the trees
It is the ineffable mystery
that walks through my door and sits
down beside me in my loneliness
for the sweetest cup of misery

Wish

Why wish for anything less
than to be blessed with the grace
you have given – given in return.
Why wish for anything more
than the accumulation of before
mysteriously bestowed, a hand,
a heart, a kind glance that snaps
the stars back into alignment.

You become what you behold
and behold what you've become.
The sum of your experience
is perception – kindness is
a practice; love is a way.

What comes from beyond
this growth of sentience
spins in infinite mystery.

Forgiveness

When forgiveness finally
came after the aching nights
where the moon was a bruise
and the stars were smothered
with black gauze and the dreams
shook you from your sleep and hate
was a thought that rolled over in your head
and you sank in your bed like quicksand
and pulled your way out long before dawn

Forgiveness had been a conundrum
a word a wish but nothing more
than a notion under that spell
that clutched you from the past
and held you back from being blessed
by the new day and the ones who
stood to wipe your tears away

Forgiveness was a blue day
of unencumbered sunshine
of blessing all that was behind
in the most unselfish way
the memory of old friends
and your years of comradery
who spat on your dissent
and walked the other way
and your profession where you

plied your art with heart and soul
stripped from you like a frock
because you would not take a knee
and bow before their authority.

All the icing on that old cake
blessed and forgiven for slipping
away like youth to old age
or the loss of loved ones
to that great mystery

Forgiveness was a yes when it came
the first thought after waking up
from the dream blessed
with a love that was born for giving

The Spark

Before the brain found thought
we lived in a world we've forgot
where spirits commingle still
and all is one at once

We must have known
this love that has blown
inconstant as a breeze

We must have felt the ecstasy
in the vibrant air between
where syllables like bubbles pop
beyond the reach of poetry

Before the mind had fallen
and attached itself to clay
we must have flown above
it all on delicate wings

The veils of consciousness
the five senses and flat thought
do not have the levity
to see what we've forgot

Our spirits in the clay
a mouth and hands begot
that we might make some permanence
in the world that was not

that we might lift the day
from the cauldron of the dark
that we might wake the flesh
of earth with the living spark

Growing Old

I have met and known old people
who have grown beyond suffering and loss,
the broken heart, the prodigal child,
death to those they held so close.

I have seen in their wise eyes
all of it spinning as the earth
turns in its diurnal course.

I have seen a levity in their
smiles floating in thin air.

I have seen unselfishness
in their patience to sit and hear
my indignation and rage
against the folly of our age.

I have known them to go through
such pain on the hospital bed
rising above the dying flame
affirming a love for those who remain.

I have known them to go through years
of battling death beyond prediction
creating exquisite art or solving
complex math equations.

I have seen them, I have known them
to float above the decaying house
and the overgrown field and farm.

I have seen through their wise eyes
the spinning world and what exists
beyond it all and expands into soul.

I have known there can be
wisdom in growing old.

Hands

High in the hills she is fed
and by the quiet she is led
into the reach of hands beyond

The unfolding trees
the innocence she sees
everywhere nature abounds

The thrust of the sea
and blustery wind -
whispers sink into sand
inscrutable tidings and
enticements from the hands
of the sea to the land

She is fed her spirit spreads
to all the four horizons
The great presence of the sea
the spirit through all things
surface to her understanding

She is led we are led
by hands of an invisible guide
How we know and where we'll go
becomes a kind of calling

We learn to feed as we are fed

this invisible gift of the friend

She prepares her feast

her moveable retreat

for all with an open hand

The Cold Quiet

The windows gaze at snow
Days and days we watched it fall
from clouds we could not see
It came like an invasion
thousands of flakes
some an early sacrifice
while others began to stick

white on white from the bone
bright air a foot thick
We walked everywhere we went
wrapped in scarves and layers

We were searching for something
more than the food we bought
Even at the grocery store we took
pictures of the white wonder

We rolled it into human form
We assailed it with questions
as if it could reply
We altered our perception
and gave it another try

There was some austere beauty
even a purity perhaps
as the woods in the ravine
put a finger to its lips and
reveled in the cold white quiet

Water

Water knows no creed
no word to bend the knee
no right to make us bleed

Water swishes and washes
through each and every thing
We are soaked with its magic
without even knowing

Water pours water flows
There is no end to its wandering
River to lake and lake to sea
from sea to sky from God to me
rushing through my veins
and over the rocks
and out through my skin
Water talks of glimmering
night under moonlight
flashes of brilliance through day
Water winds and finds
its own way

There are those who pretend
they can make water obey
They build dams and dikes

They build walls with spite
but water refuses to
submit to their sway

It just waits to rise
or roll away
into the arms
of another day
Water like spirit
teaches the way

Topanga Beach

The rose red hues
of late afternoon diffuse
everywhere you turn your gaze

a sense of suspension wings
above the water with the heart
reflected in the great glass mirror

Beauty is a feeling beyond
the perception of vibrant colors
mixing in the momentary air

Beauty comes from somewhere
far within where dancers start
around a fire and chants begin
to beat the rhythms of the heart

It is the practice of such perception
to exceed itself in transformation
of ancient blood into spirit

that calls us from our doubt
and the waves of confusion
to that communion we can
begin to call a kind of love

We diet on beauty
and its sweet apprehension
through long walks and dreams
of mystical proportions

We breathe and meditate
on its subtle suggestions
and surrender like sails
careening to its sway

Wave After Wave

When I think of what falls away
I start to think of what's coming forth

At Zuma Beach wave after wave
tumbles at my feet then
sucks back into the sea

The gulls surround me
like little beggars with nothing
else to do but wait

I will take what is given
a stone a shell a pearl

whatever unfurls a lover
a friend a new beginning
after the math of the end

Death waits like the beggar gulls
to pluck my skin from my bones

The spirit rises like sand
in the wind and blows
somewhere to begin again

What I hold dear for now is mine
borrowed from some
inscrutable design

I celebrate the feast
of blood and wine
and the sacraments of the flesh

The sun on the horizon
bleeding across time spreads
its fantail of fiery red

and drops like a stone
over the edge as it ushers
the dark into my bed

When I think of what's falling away
I have to think of what's coming forth

Like horses galloping
through dew toward day
or my grandsons at play

love finds me again

This is all I am both
the beginning and the end
greeting each other in passing

like a blessing wave after wave

Early Morning Light

Stars spinning in the milk moonlight,
late night wandering to the cadence
of the heart, I wish for an angel
to whisper in tongues of dark green leaves,
or through the wash of waves from the sea
across the expanded spinning body.

Follow your bliss to her or him
or neither in the nuclear fusion
of mind and space as one,

the gentle embrace of the mountain
grass where you fall into arms
beyond thought or touch.

You may shape your mind
into a fresh new painting
still dripping with the annunciation
of a starry night where the lover
was discovered in the breathing grass,
in the hands of the friend,
in the glance of the stranger
who beckoned down dizzy streets
into bustling bars where the nectar
for a moment made you feel complete.

You wake beyond what you had imagined
as your basic human right to create
recreates the borders of the body
through wild math or divination,
through your embrace of the other,
nation, brother, sister, lover.
You write your new name and remake
the body electric into a freedom that
surpasses slander and petty moral fetters,
and the old chipped paint on the night.

The expansion is spring loaded;
the awakening in the morning dew
is contagious birth upon birth.
The soul has spoken through
long meditations with the ocean
and these late night rambles
and wavering walks through the sun-
struck foothills above the City of Angels.

Transparent Sky

What is yet to write
is what I do not know
Where it will come from
and why is why I gaze
into the emptiness
and wait for a reply

I believe in the voices
faceless and noiseless
that have come will come
to say the next step
to take along the way

I believe in the people
stranger or friend often
stranger that will come
and brush my wing and
stir my pot of poetry

They say take my hand
and follow these words
like breadcrumbs back
into the living light
horns honking in the street
children shouting at play
the day bounding
and blessing everything

Everything is blessed
with the invisible touch
with the harmony of syllables
forming around what cannot
be said but flowers in the head
lotus like and numinous
the luminous morning

There will be wrinkled skin
and broken hearts that
will not mend again
An old woman may die alone
bereft of family and friend

Corruption may steep
contagion in the stew
and evil will crawl from under
the rocks and take on proportions
that cannot be stopped

If we but listen though
beyond all that is born to rot
the whisper ineffable
the invisible hand
like the inexplicable nature
of a love that transcends
our selfish demands will lead

to the next door the next
illusion in the dream
that lifts us higher and deeper
than we can possibly think
until the emptiness is clarity
and all we'll ever need
For everything was always
and already here
Dorothy in Kansas need not
click her heels for home
was always right where
she was sleeping

It's hard to imagine
made of dirt and bone
the whole universe is spinning
right where we stand
on the head of a pen
that spills out these words
like a hive full of honey
like a transparent sky
where we can revel in the senses
or look straight into the eye
beyond what we can imagine

The Mission

I look through stained glass windows
to see the light from many views

Every day the child is born
with the spirit shining through

Through all these colors this innocence
is born and recalls us to our essence

When we give to the hungry
when we give to the afflicted

this child appears shining bright
this child again born from the light

When I look at all the images
that are carefully carved in stone

the nativity with the child and the lamb
the crucifixion that happens with every

man or woman who has discovered
the sacrament of living for others

I see the gravestone rolled aside
and the ascent of man from inside

The resurrection rises every morning
as our eyes return to the light of day

We know then why we were put here
to rise above suffering and decay

to learn to give what we can't afford
to learn to listen for the sacred word

that whispers so softly in the silence
and rolls within on waves of the sea

Some say ancient scrolls harbor divinity
while this need to write aches and bleeds

Here at the Mission I kneel and pray
to be forgiven and to give love today

The heart beyond our own suffering
lifts the soul to the great horizon

where the views of many colors
through the stained glass clear

and all the separate faiths
part from fractious fighting

and in one last act of judgment
merge into expansive vision

of one and all spirits rising

The Offering

What if like stars we turned
inside out and you could see
the light exploding through the dark

What if when you finally see me
your eyes begin to spin toward infinity

What if the birds that sing
bring the light up every morning

What if the light you love
is the light within and the light above

What if the light I can see
in your compassionate imagery
ignites a vibrant spark in me

What then if the heart begins
to open from within like a rose

What then what if what rises
from the sweet light we compose

spills its luminous offering
on all that gives and grows

On all that gives and grows
on all we think we know
the rising light of love bestows

Oneness

Now and Then

Where have all these people gone?
The tide rolls in its salient song.
I look within and they're still young
and vibrant as the sun
with its long tongue of light
that licks across the sea
from the horizon
to the stone at my feet.

I can see them, feel them,
love them still and wonder
if they can still feel what
we felt where they are
and where they were
as I do now and
then where I am.

Ocean Green

The ocean green in successive waves
recalls again the repetition
and continual advance of difference,
the tide in redisposition,
of the grains of sand,
the shifting land where we stand,
the wash of cells, the approach
of age and ages yet to come.

The ocean beats its percussive drum
in waves that wash like struck cymbal,
like the eternal ohm, again and again,
the whisper of foam at our feet,

the language of the universe
tuned by the magnetism of moon
and star, spun on the finger
of something larger, infinitely out there
and infinitely within each particle,
each grain of sand, each individual man,
spun on the finger, washed to the shore,

rearranging the beach, the mind,
to repeat the eternal difference of each
and every report of a singular voice.

Eclipse

With a late morning moon
veiling the sun, cookie cutter
patterns of crescent light
look like a flock of crows
penetrating shadows of leaves.

The songbirds treble from the trees again
as if the day has just begun to shine
when the air snaps crisp and cold.

Goose bumps form on my arms as my
students bounce around like bunnies
and share their funky glasses
and cardboard boxes to stare
at the disappearing sun.

The eclipse is nearly one
as I become all yours
and you become all mine.
Everyone grows dizzy
with the phenomenon
as we toast some new unity
and the day which is still
young remains undone.

Play

Each time we pass the playground
the laughter and shrill cries

children running crisscross
like zipping bees around a hive

the unbridled thrill of horses bucking
and galloping on the endless plain

Hawks swoop from the treetops
A shy deer hides in the shade

The play appears so pure
a fresh and tumbling cascade

a reminder of what we've forgotten
in the contracts that we've made

The children in the playground
with the fluid dance of play

dash away from tomorrow
in the golden promise of today

The Still Life Café

At the Still Life Café
I get stuck on the words.
In still life portraits objects
pose for hours just to be
rendered in the right light
with the full lengths of their shadows.
Pears and peaches coupled up
like lovers at a table,
I can see them gazing into the other
incapable of uttering
their ripened passion.

Or maybe still life might refer
to the fact that life
still goes on here every day
feet flowing through the door
hands reaching out for a hot latté
eyes lifting up into the absence of you
without a sharp recognition of the loss.

I know this place as our rendezvous
where we talked about poetry
and the art behind the act of seeing.
We would climb the narrow stairs
to your studio at the corner window,
and you would show me the forms

that had coalesced in your head,
numbers that had grown intricate
proportions and yielded to your hands.

When we surveyed the frescos
of the building across the street,
you would tune my eyes
to their deep structure
press them through texture and shape
into the print of some delicate finger
reaching out of the inaudible other.

I could never quite see
what you were trying to show to me;
I imagined fractal perfection,
like replication in a snowflake,

your art hanging suspended
in a space on the wall
while all the world swept through
possibility incinerating like a match.

I wondered if you had melded
your imagination to this
infinite existence that numbers
and words could only begin to address.

Your boyish smile would put
everything in its place;
there could be no regret.

I sip the warmth from this cup
then set the circle
within the circle of the saucer
and remember what I loved best.
With the soup on your shirt,
and a crumb in your smile,
you would chuckle from your belly
on this side of perfection
as you watched the children whirl
through their passions and rise up
like angels into permanent blue.

Faces

I look up at the coffee shop
after hours of writing and see
so many faces I remember
although we have probably
never spoken and I begin
to wonder what I am forgetting

Is it a student of mine or a
father of one from long ago
I immediately feel a connection
one they may never even know

The flood of faces rolling by
like watching a river flow
I'm sure I've seen this woman
but she was that young years ago

The water keeps on rolling
undulating through the stones
and I know I've seen these banks
before when I touch the ground

Every glimmer seems familiar
a kind of deja vu I presume
and wonder if I started talking

to almost anyone in the room
if we might begin to remember
some time we shared together
or some moment yet to come

I don't know how all this fits
within the bigger picture
but I am happy to see
so many faces everywhere
have become a part of me

The United State

That which unites us all,
let's write it down and get it right,
so that those inclined to misconstrue
can see themselves as well and might
resist the urge to martyr our words.

I see you love your children,
your parents, even your dog.
Your generosity to a brother,
a friend or just someone in need,
each of these do not go unnoticed.

Your grief over the loss of a mother,
or a neighbor – your appreciation
for beauty and grace – your integrity,
your loyalty, each and every trace
of your sense of compassion for another,
I celebrate! I extol! I will fight
for your right to keep another whole.

Your expertise, your art and what
you construct; your humor, your eloquence,
your dance, your faith in something greater
and your humility before all of that;

your heights, your vision beyond
selfishness, your expanded identity
beyond some reductive stance;

your humanity, your soul above
and beyond how others might malign
or attempt to control what you are
and who you can become; your love
of those who are beyond or apart
from the reach of your vision;

your pain, your despair, your sweat,
your fierce refusal to submit;
your spirit, your magic, your mystery.

I celebrate all for their novelty,
their difference and their expansion
of what I see as me and everyone
who joins in this communion
of distinct and personal humanity.

One World

My spirit and yours
everywhere celebrate
the new bud blossoming

From winter we came
wrapped around each other
warding off the cold.

Through summer, through fall,
it all spins round and round,
seasoning through the seasons.

We come through, sweet,
gentle, wise, and strong.
Me and you, we come through

it all, wrapped around
each other into one world.

Green Lake Loop

The tree tops dipped in blue,
clouds frothy plump with drink,
seagulls call your secret name
and sail the day on the wind.

The same people it seems
circle around the lake.
Wheels spin and whisper meek
prayers as they pass away.

A young child and an old man
walk together in the same shoes.
You wonder who's behind
and who's ahead of who.

If time's like a circle,
from life to death we wake
and dream with each return
the end we wish to make.

Walking around the lake
together hand in hand,
we discover with the lover
no beginning and no end.

Starry Night

In that small town
with its lone steeple
and its steady people
tucking in for the night,

one hand stands apart
and paints the night sky
with what the eye can
see drunk on divinity.

Whirling blues and oranges
churn the spheres above,
rumbling and resonant noises
conducted by the brush.

Within this vibrant orchestration,
symphonic above the quiet town
and full of a sense of wonder
that none below had found,

the people are caught beneath
their steeple and the cypress tree
inside their rows of houses
and the planted symmetry.

None received this sacrament
that murmurs above us to this day
that Vincent through his sacrifice
opened up the heavens' gate.

The Nightingale Song

Let the Nightingale sing
his own self to please
He was never born to pour
his deep throated ease
into ears of some bureaucracy

The warble of the words
the sweet swoon in your ear
the dizzy dropping syllables
of the solitary bird were

overheard in ancient times
called the lovers to embrace
and touched the soul divine
in the secret quiet space

The Aristotelian distinctions
the categories that put in place
this people from that people
do not discern the individual voice

the rapture of music
of poetry and love
the whispers from within
a song from the bough above

In the dark the deep chaunt
from that brilliant Bird
who would ever imagine
had they not stopped and heard
the florid shades of the woods
the velvet notes of the word

That Horse

That horse you rode
on the whistling wind
on the foam of a wave
That horse you rode
that burst flower into flame
the one that many knew
but no one had seen
that many tried to give a name
with the power of poetry
or the rapture of song

That horse you rode
that rumbled like thunder
through the thick of the clouds
and crushed to dust
the dreams of the crowd
as the frivolous few
clung to a shroud
of the words they were sure
were the Word from you

Many will remember
as you sat proud
that horse you rode
bold and forbidden
that bounded beyond
the years to come and
what is yet to be written

Muses by Moonlight

Who are you that I reach out
with my pen through the page
to extend our conversation and rave
about the marvels on the beach
the thick moss grown green

on the storm bent trees
and the struggle that takes us
to our knees to pray for guidance
beyond servility or constant craving

The sea speaks a language that translates
to me impermanence and mystery
the endlessness of space
spread wide as the eyes can see
and above the winking stars
and the hush of night calling
us even further into wonder

This driftwood gift I place
in the fire beside you crackles
and hums a tune in your ear
The stars the wash of shells
on the shore the fire that burns
like the heart when it starts
to understand a love that brings
it all so close that we hold it tight

and whisper our most delicate words
that slip into syllables of the sea
lapping and lisping what we can only feel

There is still more to say here
about how we come together
magnetic moon and ocean and
who you are that I reach out tonight
to hold you tight and let you drift
and wonder at your return and the gifts
you leave in the sifting sands

The Stick

The stick that broke in two
became me and you
It broke clean through
like bone through marrow
and one arm grew
and then another
From one leg there were two
and we learned to walk together
When one spoke another knew
their reflection in the other
and it grew into mother father
sister brother lover friend
until the end of neither

Father

I walk and I feel my father's
steps his dust in my dust

I talk and I hear my father's
voice his timbre in my tone

I know that I am never alone
and when I'm dead I won't be gone

Is it blood to blood that carries
us along or do we belong

to something more than dust to dust
I sing my song for more than me alone

To what is it that we belong
the spirit of man and the great throng

or is it the dirt of the earth
or the salt of the seas and oceans

My mind travels the galaxies beyond
the windows and mirrors of every sun

to each and every one I meet
the steps of my father in my own feet

the love of my brother in our defeat

the voice of the enemy in my own song

and the universe to which we belong

and the spirit that leads to the father beyond

Mother

She brought God down close to earth.
"The animals are better than people," she said,
and the animals knew she meant it.
The birds heard the word and clustered
in her trees as the raccoon and deer nestled near.

She would stay awake through the darkest
nights to talk us through our loss of sight.
A hand, a ride, something deep inside
drove her to deliver us and more,
the other children who came to her door.

She raised us to believe in the first light,
that the sun itself was the gift of life,
that flowers and trees, shrubs and weeds
were all the children of his delight.
His presence knelt beside her in church;
she brought God down close to earth

As children we thought she might be a witch.
What is bad, who to trust, what we did
in the dark of night out of sight, we thought
she simply knew too much.

Unselfish acts through suffering,
a condition she knew so well,
she would bring the spirit within reach
to catch each child before they fell.

Now the loss of her from our world
is a gaping hole we must fill.
She has gone back to earth
and beyond the wind with her will.
By her example we must learn
to give more than we take

and heed the word she must have heard
that brought God down so close
our souls began to wake.